WITH LOVE

Made in the USA
Monee, IL
14 June 2021

71250586R00046